GANGSTER
TO
GOD

From Prison Gang to God's Gang

TIMOTHY RAU

WESTBOW
PRESS®
A DIVISION OF THOMAS NELSON
& ZONDERVAN

WestBow Press books may be ordered through booksellers or by contacting:

WestBow Press
A Division of Thomas Nelson & Zondervan
1663 Liberty Drive
Bloomington, IN 47403
www.westbowpress.com
844-714-3454

Scripture taken from the New King James Version® Copyright © 1982
by Thomas Nelson. Used by permission. All rights reserved.

ISBN: 978-1-6642-1323-4 (sc)
ISBN: 978-1-6642-1324-1 (e)

Library of Congress Control Number: 2020923196

Print information available on the last page.

WestBow Press rev. date: 01/05/2021

To My Perfect and Wonderful Father and To My Lord and Savior Jesus Christ, I am eternally grateful for the incredible Love and Amazing Grace you have shown me, and for all the ways you have changed my life.

And to my Beautiful and Amazing Wife Micaela Rau, and two Precious Children Hannah and Christian who are a gift from Heaven. I love you and am so grateful to God for you.

Love Never Fails.....

INTRODUCTION

FREEDOM.....July 2, 2008. Hello, my name is Timothy Adam Rau and this is my testimony. The book you're about to read is an incredible life story, it is a Love story straight from the Heart of Father God, an amazing and wonderful Father, Who by The Power of His Love and Amazing Grace, completely turned my life around, rescuing me out of a life filled with darkness, pain, depression and drug addiction. A life that had been destroyed completely with no hope left. An amazing story of God and how He brought me out of that darkness and into a relationship with My Lord and Savior Jesus Christ and the incredible miracles that followed after He saved me.

By the world's view and overwhelming odds against me, I would have become just another statistic, a lost cause, a lost soul, but God proved that nothing is impossible to Him and to those who believe. I became a new creation in Jesus Christ, overcoming things that were absolutely impossible to overcome, things that had held me in chains from becoming the man He planned for me to be. By His Grace and Saving Power, the odds against me were removed and I became another success story not of my own making but by what only Jesus Christ could do in my life and by Him, I was given a second chance, filled with hope and a future to do what I never dreamed possible. The last twelve years of what happened to me and things I witnessed are recorded in this book so you can see how my life was radically changed forever because of His Love, and how other's lives were changed as well.

To outsiders looking in, I grew up with a seemingly normal life, attending Sunday School, being enrolled in Christian private schools from kindergarten until the seventh grade. My life was far from normal though. I was a very confused and hurt child. My mom who was battling drug and alcohol addiction abandoned us and left our home and our family far behind when I was four years old, and for the most part, was absent from our lives over the next eleven years. I remember there being a whole lot of violence and chaos in our home growing up, along with drugs and alcohol. I was very afraid of things that were taking place in my life, which no child should ever have to experience, things that I could not control, and never should have been exposed to. I also remember there were good times when I felt safe and was very happy, the years when I was attending Christian school and in Church.

The years where I was loved and taught by Christian men and women who knew God, who nurtured me and helped me along in my early years, people who spoke into my life and taught me about The Lord Jesus Christ and how much He loved me. At home, it was a very different story though. At the age of eight, I had already been introduced to marijuana and alcohol and things I should never have been exposed to. These were two very different worlds I knew and grew up in and the one that meant the most to me, where I belonged and where I was safe, would be left far behind, a faded memory as I grew older and because of the tragedies that were about to take place in my life. For the next twenty-two years using drugs and alcohol would become my reality, and a sure destructive way I would escape the pain I was about to endure as I hit my teenage years. I lost five family members from 1984 to 1987.

I was eleven years old when tragedy struck for the first time, my Grandfather Talbot Trevethan, who I was very close to, lost his life to cancer, and two years later in 1985, my Grandmother Marjorie passed away after spending a short period of time in a convalescent home. The worst of all these tragedies and a real turning point in my life happened in 1986 when my brother Brian, who was my best friend, who I loved with all my heart, was stabbed and killed while committing a crime, high on drugs. He was only 20 years old. It was by far the most painful thing I had ever felt and after that, the next few years would soon become the darkest years of my childhood as one after another, the people who I loved, lost their lives. I fell into severe depression during those years that I could not overcome. My brother Brian had battled drug and alcohol addiction from an early age and was never able to get a grip on his life.

Five months after my brother was killed my stepmom Shirley whom I was very close to died also, from lung cancer, and six months after that my mom was taken and died from cancer (a brain tumor). At that point, I had totally lost my will to live and stopped caring about life altogether. I turned to a life of alcohol and drug addiction, to escape my depression, not knowing how much destruction it would cause me as the years went on. I lost all touch with Christianity, and Jesus became just a faded distant memory. As I grew older I believed that Jesus Christ was just a fairytale, a story that adults told us children, to make us happy like the story of Santa Claus. He had been the only life I had ever really known where I felt safe, that brought me any kind of happiness as a child. After all the tragedy and death, I had no answers and I was left to figure out on m own why all these things had happened to me.

My depression became so unbearable and my life so hopeless that year after year my addiction progressed and got worse as I continued to spiral downward into despair. I used drugs daily to escape my reality, and the more I tried to escape my pain, tried to fix myself, the worse things got for me and the angrier and confused I became because of it. I rebelled against all authority and completely turned away from all the good people in my life that wanted to help me. I began getting in trouble with the law, committing the same crimes that got my brother killed years earlier. I first ended up in the juvenile hall at the age of 14, and then at 23 my first time in jail and finally ending up in prison where my anger would be turned into hatred and I would become a violent gang member, someone Jesus never intended me to be.

I moved to Arizona in 1993, trying to get clean and a handle on my life, but after only a few months I lost my fight and fell back into the drug addiction I so much despised. I was arrested two different times which landed me in Maricopa County Jail for a couple of short stays but that wasn't enough for me to stop. I was not strong enough to overcome my issues and by my third arrest in 1995 I was facing three and a half years in prison, that's when the superior court in Phoenix Arizona gave me an alternative. Instead of a three-year prison term, they offered me one year in a program called Teen Challenge. I had no idea what Teen Challenge was but I took their offer knowing it would get me out of going to prison for three years. After waiting a few months in jail I was released to enter the program.

The Lord was trying to save my life and spare me from any more destruction, but I had no clue that it was God making these things happen in my favor, and I ran. I made another horrible mistake by leaving Teen Challenge only a couple of days after my arrival because I was now on the run from the law and going to prison for sure. For months I was hiding on the streets of Phoenix Arizona, ducking and dodging police at every turn, and one night a few months later, two guys I had met on Van Buren Street, who I had been getting high with, gave me a stolen van which they had pulled an armed robbery in the night before at a motel room, kidnapping a guy and robbing him, taking off with his van.

I ended up in possession of the van later the next day and in a string of horrible choices I was making during my drug addiction, it all finally caught up with me when I was arrested and charged with a string of car thefts that I had done and then two weeks later charged with the armed robbery and kidnapping that was committed in the van fell on me. After sitting in jail for two weeks I was called to court at four in the morning to be arraigned for these new charges. The judge read the charges filed against me and I was shocked to learn after speaking to my public defender I was facing 30 to 45 years in prison if I took these charges to trial and lost.

All my bad choices had finally caught up with me, it was a complete nightmare becoming my reality. There was no way for me to prove my innocence, I was told by my public defender if I went to trial the district attorney would bury me because they claimed the victim had pointed me out in a photo lineup as the guy with the gun. I was railroaded by the state of Arizona justice system and even after pleading to my public defender that I knew the car was stolen and there was no way I could have been pointed out in a photo lineup because it was not me, that I looked nothing like the guys I got the vehicle from, one being Hispanic and the other Black, he still advised me that I wouldn't win in trial.

I had no choice but to sign a "no contest" plea agreement for ten and a half years that the district attorney had offered me, instead of taking a chance on a jury trial. On my sentencing day, I stood up in front of the judge and told him I was guilty of being in possession of a car I knew was stolen but they were sending me to prison for a crime I did not commit. The judge stated I had signed the plea agreement and there was nothing he could do but sentence me to what I had agreed to. I spent the next ten years of my life in prison, from 1997 to 2006.

Survival of the fittest in that world, to stay alive, I became a gang member, doing everything I was asked to do to show my loyalty and to survive. I spent three different terms in lockdown while in prison, in complete solitary confinement, a year or more at a time because of things I had to do. I endured loneliness and the extreme stress of being confined to a tiny 12x6 cell with only three hours outside three times a week. I was able to keep my sanity by doing push-ups and pacing back and forth in my cell for hours every day as I waited for each meal to be slid through a square slot in my steel door.

No matter what the punishment from prison guards and officials I learned real quick in prison that you had to be strong no matter what the cost and do whatever you were asked to do by the older convicts no matter where it sent you. I started my time locked down in a Supermax Prison Facility called SMU in Florence Arizona and then moved on from there to high-level prison yards where I was being groomed to be a vicious killer, around the most violent and dangerous men society had to offer.

Stabbings, brutal assaults, and even death were a normal part of everyday life in prison, a place filled with so much darkness and hatred, where there was very little hope at all if any. Everyday life inside was sometimes unbearable as lockdowns and searches for weapons left us in handcuffs all hours of the night until early morning hours, officers searching for a knife used in a stabbing or drugs that were brought in which we used to make money and numb ourselves from the horrible reality of our world inside.

In 2001, four years into my prison term, tragedy struck my life again as my dad who I loved dearly and was all I had left, died of ALS (Lou Gehrig's Disease) at the age of 64. My dad was the one person who was always there for me no matter what happened. I loved him with all my heart and it was another horrible battle I had to face, trying to deal with his death in a place where you never show any kind of weakness or emotion. It was one of the hardest things I had to go through during my time in prison and it took me further into my drug addiction and darkness, shooting up meth and heroin as an escape from my pain.

The year 2006 arrived and my ten-year sentence was over and I was finally released from prison. I had survived the hardest ten years of my life and made it out without a scratch because of My Father and Lord Jesus, Who I had no idea had been watching over me the entire time, Who I know now had made sure I was safe every moment that I was behind bars. When I got home I was completely institutionalized and felt so lost, the real world that I had not been a part of for so long was very different. I had been frozen in time and thrown back into the world 10 years later with no idea how to live a normal life and I was left all alone to try to figure it out.

I had major PTSD and I was having an extremely hard time adjusting, not knowing how to make it outside of the prison walls I called home, not knowing how to survive in the real world. I was living in a place I no longer knew, with no hope of ever being normal, still living in darkness without The Lord. I tried my best to get it together but mentally I battled day after day to try to hold it together. I finally caught a break a few months after my release and got a job working in a furniture warehouse, but after only eight months I was still struggling and fell. I was back on drugs and back in prison again for a year violation. I was released again in the later part of 2007 but no matter how hard I tried to make it I continued to fall and In May 2008 I lost hope and gave up completely going back to drugs again and committing crimes to fuel my addiction.

I was arrested and charged with another felony in May 2008 and as I sat in Ventura County Jail in California I awaited my fate. This time when I went to court I was called to appear before the judge and told by my public defender it was the last time I would ever be free. It was by far the worst news anyone could ever imagine, as the public defender told me that I was being struck out by the state of California, that this case was my third strike, and I was going to be spending the rest of my life in prison, my life was over. I sunk in my chair, my heart was broken beyond anything I had ever felt before.

I had nothing more to lose, my life was completely over. I would never see the light of day again outside of prison walls, and all I could think every day was that I would never see the real world again, that I would never have a family, or experience the happiness I so longed for in this life. My fight was now over, I was going to die in prison, an old bitter man who threw his life away, and that when I finally died there was nothing after that.

It completely broke my spirit and I began to have thoughts of committing suicide, rather than be locked up for the rest of my life. I had done too much time already and didn't want to live that way anymore. It seemed at that time my only option was to just end it all, to take myself out of my misery but The Lord had a different ending to this story.

While I was in jail, living in the cell next to me was a guy who grew up in the same town as I had. He was a Christian and when I told him what had happened to me he said that if I would pray and ask God for help, Jesus would help me. I didn't believe what he was saying, I had heard the same thing my whole life and all I could think or say to him was that I didn't need God, and what I needed was a lawyer to get me out of the mess I was in. A few days went by, stressful day after day trying to call people for help without success. I had no one and every day I would end up even more depressed about my situation because I had no one to help me. Then one morning the daily newspaper which the cell block would pass around and share every morning was slid under my door. I read about a jail inmate who had just committed suicide a few days earlier right next door to the cellblock where I was housed.

I began to think about how I could do the same, how I wanted my life to end as his life had. I thought about how I would tie a bed sheet around my bunk and just end it all, and that my misery would be over for good. That same morning after our cell doors popped opened for our 1 hour time out of our cells, I walked down the stairs with a broken heart, having exhausted every idea I could come up with to escape this nightmare I was trapped in when I looked over to a table and saw one book sitting there, a book with a green cover and a tree on the front, a book that for some reason I had seen many times the last few years. I read the cover and it was as if a light switch turned on. It was "The Purpose Driven Life" by Rick Warren.

I had no idea that life as I knew it was about to be changed forever from that very moment on and this moment in time was the beginning of my new journey through life because of a God and Father Who had written a different story than the one that was going through my head. I was now about to meet my Father, Who loved me deeply and cared about my situation. He was about to do something that I never dreamed or imagined could be possible.....I stared at the book, knowing it was not a coincidence that it sitting right there for me to find and I instantly remembered back in 2003 when I had a neighbor in prison who was also a Christian.

His name was Brian and he had tried a few times to talk to me about God, and once offered me this same book, trying to get me to read it so that I could know what He knew was the truth of Who Jesus is. I was too caught up in the politics of prison and gang life at that point to even consider anything he was saying though, but that night five years later when I picked that book up off that table in that county jail, after everything that was happening in my life, I knew the word coincidence was more than just a word, and that's when The Lord began to open my eyes to see Who He is and began to speak to me about a plan and future that He wrote for me, that I was not a mistake, that every moment of my life He was there with me and all I had to do was believe and trust Him.

He was about to set me free, and I was completely blown away because I knew without a doubt that God My Father and The Lord Jesus were absolutely one hundred percent real and I was not alone there in that place. I knew that He did have a plan for my life and that good plan was about to begin. Only God could have orchestrated these things and the way they were happening. That first night, in that county Jail I went back to my cell and began to read, and after a few days, on July 2, 2008, I prayed and asked God to forgive me, and asked Jesus to save my life. The most profound thing that has ever happened to me in my entire life came alive in me at that very moment and I was filled with The Holy Spirit Of God.

I wept tears that I had kept inside for so many years, for all the pain I had carried and endured, for every wrong I had ever done, and for the way I had lived my life. I wept tears of joy that I had never experienced before and Jesus completely set me free. Jesus freed me from all that was weighing me down, freed me from my past, freed me from the darkness that had consumed my life, and from everything that was hurting me inside, everything that was holding me in chains was broken. I had been told by doctors all my life that I was bi-polar and a manic depressive, that I needed to be on medications because of a chemical imbalance, He freed me from that. He freed me from every label that had been placed on me that I could not escape.

For so many years I used drugs because of my issues, because of no self-worth. I had medicated and numbed the pain away for so many years to try to correct what was wrong with me and in one moment His Love healed me and made me whole again. I had lived with the facts of what I was labeled with for twenty-two years, never believing I would be normal or feel normal like other people did unless I was high on some kind of drug, but the day I gave my life to Jesus Christ was the day He began to change me and I am free today from chronic depression and many other issues because of it. Jesus touched my life and my heart that night in a way that no one ever could. He got through to me, and my life would be changed forever in the blink of an eye because of His Love for me.

My heart was softened and as I started praying and reading The Bible, I began to learn what I knew as a child growing up so long ago, that Jesus loved me and that I had a Father in Heaven who cared deeply about me and cared about my life. I began to realize that I wasn't ever alone and that Jesus had always been there with me, and never once had He forgotten me. Even in the darkest times of my life when I thought I was all alone, He was there, and He carried me through everything I went through. God was about to help me turn my life around for good and He was showing me who I really was and who I would grow to become.

God touched my life in that county jail in such a powerful way that I knew I would never be the same again. After a couple of months, God began speaking to me about Teen Challenge and I wondered why after all this time, fifteen years earlier I had run from Teen Challenge and never once thought about it after, but I realized as the months went by that God was encouraging me to go back, showing me that He had never given up and on what He had ordained and what He begins He completes. He never gave up on me, or the plan He had for my life. I'm truly grateful for that. His plan for my good was about to come to pass, a future and a hope He had always desired me to have, which included the Ministry of Teen Challenge.

After The Lord saved me I started to look back on all the years of my life, I could see very clearly His Hand had always been over my life, all the times He was there, all the times He saved me from death, and all the times He made sure I would survive. Almighty God, Master Orchestrator of all good things, Amazing and Awesome God, had me in The Palm of His Hand and I was about to embark on a journey that went beyond anything I ever imagined my life could be, beyond all my hopes and dreams. As time went on The Lords Love changed my cold and wounded heart and that hard convict that I had become died, gone forever. It Is No Longer I Who Live But Christ Living In Me, My Hope Of Glory.

The Lord found me and The Truth set me free, giving me more happiness and love than I had ever felt before in my entire life. It was total and complete freedom. I was sitting in jail facing a life sentence not knowing exactly what was gonna happen to me, and it didn't matter to me anymore. The peace of His presence in my life was more than enough, and I was freer at that moment than I had ever been since I was a child. I knew without a doubt I could trust Him and I was starting my life all over again with my Father and Best Friend by my side from that day forward.

Eight months later after many prayers, many conversations

with My Father, two promises I received from Him, promises He gave me about my situation. That everything concerning me in this court case was in His Hands, that the heart of the judge and district attorney was in His hands, and that He would turn His heart to do His Will concerning me. He assured me I had nothing to fear, and as I trusted Him going back and forth to court, I was given back my life with a second chance. Jesus said follow Me and I said I would.

The Lord knew my heart, He knew I wanted to give up that life forever and He helped me to do that. Instead of life in prison, I found mercy in that courtroom by the Grace of God. He brought the counsel of the courts against me to nothing and The Lord gave me great favor in that courtroom and freedom from the tyranny of the devil over my life. Two of my strikes were struck down, the strikes I had received in Arizona for crimes I had not committed, and I was offered a plea agreement for two and a half years in prison instead of a life sentence. It was a miracle, a gift that went beyond my understanding. The scales of my life had been weighed by The Lord and I was shown great Love and Mercy.

In July of 2009, I was released from prison and started my new life outside those prison walls forever. After already serving 8 months in jail and California's halftime, I ended up going to prison for 7 months and a year and a month later after I walked out of prison in August 2010 I was released from parole a year and 11 months early by God's Will, another miracle, and in September 2010, I entered through the doors of Teen Challenge to finish what The Lord had started in my life 15 years earlier. I graduated Teen Challenge after 14 months and in December 2011 I was given the opportunity by The Lord to attend TCMI (The Teen Challenge Ministry Institute), a one year Bible college and staff training center that prepares students for Ministry and the work of Teen Challenge, helping others with drug addiction and life-controlling issues.

While I was attending TCMI in 2012 The Lord spoke to me,

that I would have a baby girl named Hannah, that I would have the family that I had dreamed of having and prayed to ask God for. I had no idea when that would come to pass but I did know that God is Faithful and it was going to happen. I met my beautiful wife Micaela in 2012 at TCMI and had no idea then that she would be my wife 4 years later. After I graduated Bible college on December 23rd, that same year I was called by The Lord to The Teen Challenge of the Hawaiian Islands where Micaela was already working for Teen Challenge on the Big Island of Hawaii in Hilo.

I landed on Oahu in Honolulu where I would help other struggling drug addicts change their lives through the Love and Grace of Jesus Christ. In 2013 doctors told Micaela she would never have children due to a chronic medical condition called endometriosis, which she had suffered greatly since she was 12 years old. The doctors said she would never have children and tried to convince her to have a hysterectomy to remove her damaged ovaries but she refused to believe their report and did not have the procedure. The first time my wife and I were together in 2015 she conceived and five months later the doctor showed us on the sonogram that it was a baby girl. Hannah was coming, just as The Lord had promised me. The promise of My Father was coming through a woman doctors two years earlier said was barren and could not have children. Hannah Kai Rau was born in February of 2016, The Lord's promise fulfilled, a miracle showing that "All Things Are Possible With God". Then on September 19, 2017, our second miracle came with our son Christian James Rau being born.

We have 2 beautiful children now, the family I prayed for when the Lord saved me in 2008. Against all odds, Jesus Christ has done and continues to do the impossible.

My wife had a full hysterectomy in March of 2018. After removing her uterus, and her ovaries, the doctor's report confirmed the incredible odds she overcame. The report stated the uterus was so badly scared to the inside walls and so much previous damage from her condition that it was "a miracle" the doctor stated that there were no complications with either child. We praise God today knowing that He is truly The God of miracles.

My whole life and family are truly a miracle from God and an incredible story that I know is meant to give you hope and encouragement no matter what you are going through or facing right now. Against all odds, year after year as I continue my journey Home I continue to watch the Faithfulness of Jesus Christ as God helps me overcome the giants in my life one by one. God has accomplished so much in my life and as I continue to trust in Him I know for sure the best is yet to come. Better is the end than the beginning, a promise The Lord gave me a long time ago, and no matter who you are or where you've been in life, or what you have done, Jesus will help you as well. He will answer your call, saving to the uttermost those who come to God through Him. The Lord is faithful.

"Anyone Who Calls On The Lord Will Be Saved".

My life has been changed forever because of what Jesus has done for me. I went from being a 22-year drug addict, ex-convict, who was hopeless and had nothing to live for, a man whose life was completely destroyed, to a man saved by the Love and Grace of God. I was given a brand new life, and I'm living the hope and the future today I never dreamed I could have, all because of Jesus Christ.

The greatest thing in this world is to know and experience the Love and Forgiveness that God has for us when we turn to Him. He wants you to know Him. He is willing to turn your life around if you ask Him for help. The best part is He takes us any way that we come to Him. Today and every day I'm grateful that God reached out to me before it was too late.....

I am a living testimony of The Love and The Power Of Jesus Christ to save and change a life that was so completely lost without hope.

Nothing Is Impossible For God.....

"For I Know The Plans I Have For You Declares The Lord, Plans To Prosper You And Not To Harm You, Plans To Give You Hope And A Future"

- Jeremiah 29:11

THE MIRACLES

Healed Of Hepatitis C-

In 2003 after shooting up drugs and sharing tattoo needles in prison for years I began to feel a very sharp, deep pain in my right side. I was afraid to go to the doctor to find out what it was, only because many of the fellas in prison had been going to the doctor and coming back with the bad news that they were infected with the hepatitis C virus. I figured it would be more stressful for me to know that I had it than to just try to ignore the symptoms and act like it wasn't there, but after a while thinking about it everyday broke me down and I needed to find out what was wrong with me. The pains were so severe that it felt like a hot knife being shoved into my side.

I could not get comfortable, I couldn't lay down on my right side, it was horrible. So one morning I placed a medical request in the door of my prison cell. I decided to go to the doctor and have blood work done. The doctor called me back two weeks after they drew my blood for the results and said that I had a severe strain of Hepatitis C and that it was killing my liver. The doctor told me that because of the severity of the results I qualified for a prison program that would supply the liquid chemotherapy called interferon that I needed. It was not a guarantee that it would kill the virus and after watching most of the other guys take this medicine I decided not to.

These guys would become so sick they couldn't get out of bed most days I wasn't going to take my chances on something that may not even work. For five years I struggled with the pain in my side and every year it seemed to get worse and worse. In 2008 when I was facing that life sentence in prison after the Lord saved me He also miraculously healed me. When the Lord first saved me He taught me about the faith of Abraham and then He took me to the Gospels and Holy Spirit taught me about faith and healing and took me to all the scriptures where Jesus had said "your faith has made you well". At that very moment, God gave me a revelation and The Word came alive in me. Jesus gave me the faith to believe and at that very moment in that jail cell while I was reading I heard Jesus speak to me and what He was teaching me so I asked Him in faith to heal me and He did.

Eight months later in prison, I got blood work done again, and this time when the doctor called me back to give me the results he had an odd look on his face as he read the report. He asked me if I had ever taken medicine for Hepatitis C and I told him no. I told him the doctors had told me in 2003 that I had a severe case of hepatitis C and he went on to tell me that there was a marker in my blood that was evidence that I was at one time a carrier of the virus hepatitis C but that it was gone. He said to me that all my numbers were normal. I walked out of that doctor's office in tears, praising Jesus for what He had done for me. It was a miracle. It was 17 years ago in 2003 that I was told I would die from Hepatitis C and today I am healthy, alive and well, because of the healing power of Jesus Christ. I had a full physical done in 2017 and the report read nothing about hepatitis C, it is completely gone. Jesus Christ Lord of Heaven and Earth still heals today.

"For I am the LORD who heals you.'"

Exodus 15:26 NKJV

"Bless the LORD, O my soul; And all that is within me, bless His holy name! Bless the LORD, O my soul, And forget not all His benefits: Who forgives all your iniquities, Who heals all your diseases, Who redeems your life from destruction, Who crowns you with lovingkindness and tender mercies, Who satisfies your mouth with good things, So that your youth is renewed like the eagles. The LORD executes righteousness And justice for all who are oppressed."

-Psalms 103:1-6 NKJV

So Jesus answered and said, "Were there not ten cleansed? But where are the nine? Were there not any found who returned to give glory to God except this foreigner?" And He said to him, "Arise, go your way. Your faith has made you well."

-Luke 17:17-19 NKJV

THE AWESOME SOVEREIGNTY OF GOD

In 2006 after serving a ten-year prison term in the state of Arizona I was released back into society where I found myself discouraged and ready to give up on life because I could not find a place to fit in. I had filled out a couple of applications for jobs and been turned down because of my past, as you read earlier in my full testimony Armed Robbery and Kidnapping were two very serious crimes, and although there were certain companies that were known to hire felons I found after a couple of interviews that it was going to be much harder for me if not impossible to get a job. I had become very discouraged after these failed attempts to become employed and I was so institutionalized that I was fighting every day to hold on, I wanted nothing more than a chance to be a normal citizen in the outside world and so I began to use alcohol and marijuana to numb myself from the anxiety and the stress I was feeling.

I was losing hope very quickly. I was about to call my parole officer and tell him to send me back to prison where I belonged. I felt that prison was my home, the only place I would ever feel normal. And then the call came, from a lady at the parole office who helped ex-convicts get jobs. She said she had an interview for me at a Furniture Company called Zenders in Newbury Park California. I thought to myself this is going to be the last shot for me out here if I don't get the job. I went to the interview the next morning hoping I would finally catch a break. When I pulled up and got out of my car, walking up to the door of the warehouse there was a line of men there for the same job. Most of them were clean-cut and had very nice clothes on. I looked at myself all slung down with prison tattoos and I thought to myself there is no way I'm going to get hired, most of these guys probably have clean records and it's just going to be another one of those companies that turns me down because of my past.

So as I waited in line for my turn they called my name and I walked into an office and sat down with two men at a table. They asked me what my story was and I told them exactly what had happened to me 10 years earlier. That I had a horrible drug addiction, and while I was in possession of a stolen vehicle which I knew was stolen, I got arrested and charged for the theft of that vehicle, but then two weeks later while in jail I was blamed for an armed robbery and kidnapping that was committed in the vehicle that I had gotten from a couple of guys I was using drugs with. I explained that I had absolutely nothing to do with their crime but the consequences of my choices landed me in prison for ten years.

I thought for sure after telling them my story they would dismiss me and that would be the end of the interview but to my amazement, they looked at each other and the manager said I was hired, that they were going to give me a second chance. Out of all those people that were in line, all those people with a clean record, they took a chance on me and I couldn't understand why, but I was thankful and it gave me some hope. I started that Monday morning and as I worked for this company in the warehouse and as a delivery driver I became friends with the manager Paul. He asked me one day to come to his office if I wanted to have lunch with him and I said yes and as I sat down he began to talk to me about Jesus Christ. He would read a few Bible verses and we would talk for a few minutes and then I would go back to work. It was amazing because this company that hired me I realized, later on, was a Christian company and these men who hired me were showing me the love of Jesus Christ by giving me a second chance.

One Saturday I was sent on a delivery with my co-worker and as we drove up into this neighborhood we noticed that it was a very wealthy neighborhood and usually when we went on deliveries like this we would get good tips so we were really happy about this particular job. As we pulled up in front of the house a woman came out and she told us to go around the side of the house and put all the furniture on the back patio. So we put all the furniture on the back patio and were getting ready to leave when the lady came out of the front of the house and gave us both a nice tip and we were on our way. The manager had asked me a few times if I would come to his church but I always made up excuses for why I couldn't go. A few months later after a relationship, I was in ended, I went to a bar and got drunk and then relapsed back on hard drugs.

I didn't call or show up for work and when I finally got the courage to call my boss, he was very concerned for me and asked me if I was alright. He had been calling my phone and leaving messages for me, but I was already in a downward spiral and too ashamed to answer my phone. I ended up two days later going to jail, being charged with a DUI and a fight that I had got into, which sent me back to prison on violation for one year. I called my manager from LA County Jail and told him what had happened. He was still very loving and kind and asked me if I wanted to pray with him accept Christ, I said yes and after we hung up I did not pray again and when I got back to the prison yard I went back to my old life as nothing had ever happened.

I was released in 2007 and went back to being hopeless, trying to find a job, trying to find a place in this world where I couldn't fit in. It didn't take me but a month before I was hopeless again, back on hard drugs and going down fast. This time I was shooting up crystal meth and was quickly in trouble with the law again only five months after I was released from prison. I landed in Ventura

County Jail and was charged with commercial burglary and when I went to arraignment I was told it was my third strike and I would be going to prison for the rest of my life. The Lord saved me in that county jail as you read in the first part of this book, delivering me from a life sentence in prison. These are the details that happened in between.

After I got out of prison I was a new man delivered and set free by Jesus Christ. I was given a real Second Chance, everything about life was so different and I knew this time it would be for good. I called Paul the manager from the furniture company I had worked for a few years before and I told him what happened to me. He was truly amazed at what the Lord had done and told me that they had been praying for me while I was away and he was so happy to come to pick me up. We went to breakfast and then went to his Church, the same church that he had been trying to get me to go to a couple of years earlier. As I began attending Lighthouse Church, I knew that I needed something more and so I began to go to the Wednesday night celebrate recovery meetings there, a 12 step faith-based recovery program.

On one particular night, I walked through the front door of our church and I noticed that the door was closed to the meeting room where we had weekly meetings and as I tried the door it was locked. One of the youth pastors came out and told me that they had been trying to get ahold of me to tell me that the meeting had been canceled but no one had my phone number to let me know. So as I headed out the door back to my car I looked over to my left and saw a youngster about 15 years old hunched over with his hands over his eyes sitting on the curb. He was crying and as I continue to walk to my car the Lord told me to go back and talk to him. I walked up to him and asked him what was wrong.

He told me that he was part of the youth ministry there at the church but that he had been on drugs and they thought his girlfriend might be pregnant. He felt so lost without any hope of things getting better. He had told me that he ran across the freeway hoping a car would run him over. I prayed with him and I told him how Jesus had saved my life, how I had once been so lost without hope, and that Jesus had changed my life and set me free. We exchanged phone numbers that night and as the days went by we exchanged text messages. I would encourage him to trust in Jesus and we would pray together. I saw a change happening in this young man's life because of the Lord's love for him and it gave me hope for him.

One Friday night the church was having an outreach to Skid Row in Los Angeles where we would go and feed the homeless and share the love of Jesus with them. I invited Kevin to go with us and he asked me if his dad could come and that his dad was a member of the church I had not met. Kevin told me that he and his dad would pick me up and that we would drive in their car and so that night Kevin and his dad picked me up and we rode together to Hollywood to minister to the Homeless. On the way, Kevin's dad and I had a conversation about my past and I told him my testimony. I had mentioned that I had a DUI from 2006 that I was never able to take care of and that I was having a hard time getting my driver's license reinstated. He asked me what I needed to do to get it back and I told him that I had to pay an $850 fine to take DUI classes.

Kevin's dad said that he would pay the fine for me so that I could get my license back and take the DUI classes that I needed to take. I was blown away, no one had ever done anything like that for me before in my life except for my dad. I told him that I was a handyman and that I could work off the money that he was going to give me and he told me he wanted to bless me and then he went on to say that not only did he want to bless me but he wanted me to come to his house and paint his fence and asked me to let Kevin help me so that he could learn some responsibilities and that he would pay me for that as well. I agreed and Kevin's dad told me that his wife and Kevin would pick me up on Wednesday morning, that he would go buy the paint and it would all be ready for us to do that day.

So on Wednesday morning Kevin and his mom pulled up in front of my house and honked the horn. I came out and got into the car and as we started to drive to Kevin's house I started to notice something very familiar about this neighborhood that we were driving into. We pulled into the driveway of this house and immediately I was blown away by what I saw. I turned to look over at Kevin's mom and it hit me, this was the same lady that came out of the house to receive the patio furniture that I had delivered to that same house three years earlier when I was still an unbeliever working for Zenders. This young man Kevin was 12 years old playing video games up in his room that day that I delivered that patio furniture to. The Lord brought me full circle back around into their lives. And as I recounted this story to this family they were also blown away by God's goodness and by His incredible Sovereignty. It launched all of our faith to new heights as I began to realize that absolutely nothing is impossible for God. That this was just the beginning.....

""Behold, I am the LORD, the God of all flesh. Is there anything too hard for Me?"
                                        -Jeremiah 32:27 NKJV

"Now to Him who is able to do exceedingly abundantly above all that we ask or think, according to the power that works in us, to Him be glory in the church by Christ Jesus to all generations, forever and ever. Amen."
                                        -Ephesians 3:20-21 NKJV

Yours, O Lord, is The Greatness, The Power and the Glory, The Victory and the Majesty; For all that is in Heaven and in earth is Yours; Yours is the Kingdom, O Lord, And You are exalted as Head over all. Both riches and honor come from You, And You Reign over all. In Your Hand is Power and Might; In Your Hand it is to make great and to give strength to all.
                                        -I Chronicles 29:11-12 NKJV

YOUNG MOTHER
RESCUED BY THE LORD

This is the testimony of a young mother who was brought back to life by The Lord after a horrific car accident that would have for sure claimed her life had Jesus not intervened. One night in the summer of 2009 I was driving down the road after three friends and I had just got done playing pool at a local pool hall in Simi Valley CA. As I came upon the 23 freeway which was the fastest route and which I would have normally taken to get back to my house in Thousand Oaks. I would have made the turn onto the loop but something stopped me from getting on the freeway and as I continued going straight ahead I came around the bend past Moorpark Road in Thousand Oaks and started to see a whole lot of wreckage, hundreds of papers scattered across the road, a huge mess of items scattered all over the place and I pulled over quickly as I saw a Land Rover flipped over and underneath it was a young woman.

As my friend and I jumped out of the car and ran up to the woman I noticed there was complete silence, her chest was not moving at all, no sign of breathing as I stared at her lifeless body. She had a huge gash on her head and I could see the bone in her leg. The vehicle was on top of her stomach and leg. As my friend began to call 911 I felt this urgency to pray and as I prayed tears started streaming from my eyes and I remember asking the Lord to please save this Woman's life. As I continued to pray an incredible miracle happened. This young woman gasped for air and started to cry. It was amazing because I knew it was The Lord, He was there helping her. The fire trucks were pulling up and the sheriffs were asking us to get out of their way so they could do their work so we got back into our car and watched as they began to extract her from underneath the vehicle and get her into an ambulance.

When I got home it was about 12:30 a.m. and I just could not stop praying and thinking about this woman. I called the hospital to try to find out if she was okay and they told me that they could not give me any information about the accident or about the woman who was involved. So eventually I went to bed and when I woke up in the morning I continued to pray and ask God to save her. I called the hospital again to try to get any news and they told me again that they could not tell me anything. A few days went by and I continued trying to call to get any information, I wanted to hear so badly what The Lord had done. The nurse said that her family was there and that if I wanted to come down and ask for them, I could do that.

So my brother and I from church went to the hospital that night and we asked for the family and as the husband came out I explained to him how I had come across his wife that night as she lay under that vehicle. I asked him if he was a believer in Jesus Christ. He said he was not a religious man but that he knew some kind of a miracle had happened because his wife was not only up in bed but the doctors had said that she was making an incredibly fast recovery, that they could not explain. I told him about Jesus, how He had saved my life and that it was Him Who was doing this Miracle for his family. At the time of this accident, this young mother had a very young son and after a while, The Lord completely healed her and she was able to return to normal life. She is now fully recovered and has since had another child and is living a normal life, all thanks to the love and compassion of Jesus Christ Our Lord.

"The LORD your God in your midst, The Mighty One, will save; He will rejoice over you with gladness, He will quiet you with His love, He will rejoice over you with singing.""

-Zephaniah 3:17 NKJV

Jesus said, "Make room, for the girl is not dead, but sleeping."

-Matthew 9:24 NKJV

"'I am the God of Abraham, the God of Isaac, and the God of Jacob'? God is not the God of the dead, but of the living.""

-Matthew 22:32 NKJV

THE LORD SETS ME FREE AGAIN

After my release from prison in 2009, I was continually hearing about Teen Challenge and what I thought was a coincidence I began to realize after a few months That it was God was trying to get my attention but I had no interest in going into a program where I would have to be gone for another year so I kept blowing it off. I was excited about my new life in the outside world and did not want what I thought would be wasted time when I could be free. I was so confident in my new life with the Lord, but I really had no idea how things worked and that I couldn't always expect the Lord to work around my plans and as he was gentle with me I finally realized His ways are way better than my own. I was slowly learning that it was always better to follow his plans than to ever try to make up my own and follow them because His plans were awesome and full of excitement and mystery.

I made the mistake of trying to make things happen in my life that I was not ready for and in April of 2010 when I got engaged and then a few months later broken-hearted and fell into a spell of deep sadness and disappointment. In August of 2010, I was riding my mountain bike into a park with my earbuds in with the music full blast. I thought I had all the answers to my new life with Jesus but I was finding out the hard way I didn't understand what I was going to do with my life. It seemed as though nothing was going right for me and I was making mistake after mistake after mistake. I knew there had to be more to my new life with God but I didn't know how to figure I out until I pulled up to a bench in this park and I heard louder than the music the Words Teen Challenge and the name Winston.

The Lord had my attention and in my mind, I prayed and promised Him, I said Lord I give you my word if this is You and You show me that it is You I give you my word as a man I will surrender to your Will and go to Teen Challenge. As I looked on the grass in front of me about a hundred fifty feet away there was a playground with a black rod iron fence around it, and I saw a silver stamp on top showing the company that made the fence. It was about an inch long. To the left I saw a huge raven bouncing around on the grass picking the ground and I raised my hand and I said to the Lord if you make that Raven go up on that silver stamp on top of the fence I promise you, I'll go to Teen Challenge.

Winston was a brother in Christ who I had had coffee with one night and who had talked to me about Teen Challenge and asked if I would be interested in going into this program to be discipled. Little did Winston know that I had run away from Teen Challenge 15 years earlier and that God was talking to me about going back there in subtle ways the last year after saving me. So as I sat there and watched in anticipation The Raven flew up over the fence went into the playground and then turned around and flew right up on the stamp grabbing it in its claws and began to stare at me and ruffle his feathers. I was completely blown away. At that very moment, the whole world melted away and I saw God, not as a human or any words that I can even describe what I saw, but His Presence and Glory, the greatness of Who He is dropped me to my knees and I began to weep.

I felt as though I was a speck of dust in the whole universe I was so blown away it was such an experience that The Lord showed me a part of His Glory. All I could do was praise Him and thank Him, telling Him I was going to Teen Challenge. The peace that came over me knowing that I was about to embark on a journey ordained and set forth in motion by that very moment with God in that Park was going to shape the rest of my life. I immediately went home and called Winston, telling him the best I could what had just happened, the incredible news of how God spoke to me, and that I would for sure be going to Teen Challenge. Winston said he would get me in ASAP but he said the only problem was that I would have to get a parole transfer to Bakersfield California because that is where induction into the program would start, which was out of Ventura County where I was living at the time.

In the state of California in 2009 parole was a minimum of three years and I had only been on parole for one year and one month and still had a year and 11 months to go, but I knew because of the Miracles that God had already done in my life He was going to make a way for me. So after getting off the phone with Winston I called my parole officer and I got his voicemail. I left a message asking him to call me as soon as possible. The very next morning he called me and I asked him if it would be possible to do me a favor and ask the supervisor of parole if I could get a transfer to Bakersfield California so I could go into a program called Teen Challenge. He asked me if I was in trouble and I told him no I wasn't, that I just wanted to change my life.

He told me I could go anywhere I wanted because last night at midnight I was discharged off parole, one year and 11 months early and he had no explanation except he said that my release had been granted the night before, that my release card had already been sent out that morning and I was a free man. I was so blown away because God not only gave me favor but he completely set me free from anything that was holding me back in this world so that I could go where he wanted me to go. It was an awesome and incredible experience I had with the Lord that night and into the next day. It launched my faith in a way that I had never experienced before, and just as the Lord had promised me earlier on when He saved me if I believed Him like Abraham and Moses believed Him I would see His Glory. I have seen The Glory of God. Everything He has ever spoken over my life has happened just as He said it would. Jesus Is Faithful.

"The God of our Lord Jesus Christ, the Father of glory, may give to you the spirit of wisdom and revelation in the knowledge of Him, the eyes of your understanding being enlightened; that you may know what is the hope of His calling, what are the riches of the glory of His inheritance in the saints, and what is the exceeding greatness of His power toward us who believe, according to the working of His mighty power which He worked in Christ when He raised Him from the dead and seated Him at His right hand in the heavenly places, far above all principality and power and might and dominion, and every name that is named, not only in this age but also in that which is to come."

-Ephesians 1:17-21 NKJV

Therefore if the Son makes you free, you shall be free indeed.

-John 8:36 NKJV

"Lift up your eyes on high, And see who has created these things, Who brings out their host by number; He calls them all by name, By the greatness of His might and the strength of His Power; Not one is missing."

-Isaiah 40:26 NKJV

THE BLESSING
OF A CROWN

During my stay at the Teen Challenge Benedict Castle in Riverside California, I was blessed with a crown. Arriving along with other students from induction centers across Southern California in January 2011 we were put on a 30-day probationary period, where we were not allowed to go off campus like the other students who had graduated from phase one of the program. All new students had to do work there on grounds or we were put on car wash at night. I was selected for the car wash at night where we had to wake up at about 11:00 at night sometimes 1 am to go and wash cars for an auction lot that helped us raise money for the ministry of Teen Challenge there in Riverside.

About 3 weeks after I had started doing car wash, we were on break at about 2:30 in the morning where we would line up and get something to eat from one of the staff members at what we called The Snack Shack, but on this particular night I was really hungry and after eating I remembered one of the guys had given me a piece of candy so I reached into my pocket and pulled out a Jolly Rancher and when I stuck it in my mouth I bit down to crunch it up and felt something crack. It was my tooth, and it literally cracked in half. I spit out the half tooth into my hand and after rinsing my mouth out with water I was so bummed because not only did I break my tooth but all the nerve endings in my tooth were very sensitive and hurt bad.

I went off to the side and I prayed to tell the Lord there was no way that I would be able to go to the dentist and get this fixed because I didn't have insurance and I had no money. I prayed in faith reminding My Heavenly Father of His promise to supply all of my needs according to His riches in Glory through Christ Jesus My Lord and I thanked Him for helping me. It was now completely in my Father's Hands and He had taught me that by Faith, believing His Promises that I would see His Glory and promises come to pass in my life. The next day we had a student advisor meeting in the sanctuary where once a month we would meet to talk about issues we had and come up with solutions, and so I told my advisor what happened and asked him if Teen Challenge could help me with my tooth.

He told me that they had used up all the allotted money for dental that year and that I would have to wait a few months until they replenished that fund. He offered me an alternative which was to drive me down the street where there was a place that would pull the tooth for $45 and that Teen Challenge would pay for that but I didn't like that idea at all because I needed my tooth so I passed on that solution and went off to pray to the Lord again. I prayed and stated the truth, that the bottom tooth that broke I needed for eating and that I would trust and wait for Him to come through for me. A few days later I was off my probationary period, and now I would be allowed to go out and fundraise for the ministry instead of doing car wash and I was so happy to be done with that part of the program.

So the first day all loaded into the van after prayer and worship and we were off to another city to fundraise. We had little tables that we would set up in front of grocery stores telling people about our ministry and asking for donations to help in the fight against drug addiction. It was January and it was extremely cold. I was asked to get out of the van by the van leader and I was placed in front of a Smart & Final grocery store where I would fundraise from 10 am until about 6 pm. When 6 o'clock came around it was freezing cold and I kept looking for the van to pull up any second, I was in a hurry to get out of the cold into the van, where I knew that it would be warm toasty, but the Lord had other plans, and the van was running late for a reason and I was about to find out the reason why.

The last man that walked out of the store that night walked through the doors, and I asked him if he would like to make a donation to Teen Challenge. He said that he didn't have any money to give but had helped out our program in the past by doing free dental work for students in need. He was a dentist and had his own office a few blocks away from the castle. I was blown away! I told him the story about my tooth and what had happened a week before. He asked me to open my mouth so he could look at my tooth and afterward he pulled out a business card and told me to call him in a few days to set an appointment, that he would fix my tooth for me.

I called a few days later and made an appointment and Teen Challenge drove me over to his office. He took a mold of my tooth and sent it off to get a crown made. He put a temporary crown on my tooth and about two weeks later he called to tell me my permanent crown came back and he was ready to put it on me. So I went back to his office the next morning and got my crown. He said after it was a blessing and I told him I was so grateful, I had no idea how much a crown cost but I was truly grateful to The LORD My Father for doing that for me and this brother as well. God is Faithful.....

"The LORD is good to those who wait for Him, To the soul who seeks Him."

-Lamentations 3:25 NKJV

And my God shall supply all your need according to His riches in glory by Christ Jesus. Now to our God and Father be glory forever and ever. Amen.

-Philippians 4:19-20 NKJV

"It is good to give thanks to the LORD, And to sing praises to Your name, O Most High;"

-Psalms 92:1 NKJV

ENTERTAINING ANGELS

When I was a student at Teen Challenge Southern California I was sent out to fundraise at a Christian bookstore. That particular day I had woke up very tired and feeling very down, my thoughts were all over the place and I was irritated at the slightest inconvenience something that stayed with me all morning and I could not shake it. Thinking back now it was one of those days where the Lord reminded me do not think it strange the fiery trial which is to try you as though some strange thing has happened but rejoice, And count it all joy when you go through various trials knowing that the testing of your faith produces perseverance. It was the last thing I wanted to hear or go through that day but it was the truth.

I remember waking up that morning doing my daily devotion and reading the scripture that talks about Entertaining Angels. When I got dropped off for fundraising at a Christian book store I was going through it and I prayed and told the Lord how I felt, a lot of complaining and anger for how I was feeling and the last thing I wanted was to stand there for hours, I did not want to be there at all. I was seriously struggling, wanting to quit, and just be done with all of it. The store was very slow, not a whole lot of people were coming or going and it was in the very corner of a shopping center where there was hardly any traffic at all. When all of a sudden this man and this woman walk up to me and the man starts talking to me, encouraging me and then asked me if I need prayer.

I was almost in tears and I remember looking at his eyes and thinking it was very peculiar that he had the most crystal clear blue eyes I've ever seen in my life. As he started to pray for me he started to speak things over me, over my life. At that very moment, I felt the presence and peace of God and I knew this man's prayer was very powerful over me. After encouraging me the trial ended and this man and his wife walked into the store. I sat outside for about a half-hour and I started to wonder about all of what had just happened. I wanted to thank him again for helping me and eventually, I walked up to the door and poked my head in to see where he was. I looked around the store and the man and the woman were not there. I asked the person at the front counter where they had gone and they said they had no idea. I knew that they had not walked out of the front of that store because they would have had to have passed by my table.

So I sat there and wondered awhile went on with fundraising and the rest of my day. When I got home that night I had a daily devotional book that I would read at night before bed and when I opened it up I was amazed because this devotional talked about Angel's and that morning I had read in my Bible about Entertaining Angels. Right then I got a revelation and The Lord spoke to me, He opened the eyes of my understanding so clearly that He sent me that angel because of what I was going through to pray for me and to encourage me so I wouldn't give up. I was so blown away because it was one of those moments where the Lord opened my understanding and opened my ears to hear Him speak to me so clearly and to know that that is exactly what took place that day when that man came up and prayed for me.

It was so incredible to feel so loved by Jesus, that He cared about what we go through and the love that I felt from the Lord that day because of what happened I'll never forget. I was amazed He would do something like that for me in my weakness and in my trial when I was so irritated and so angry about to give up and call it quits. The Lord is faithful, He loves us so much that there are many times in our lives that without us even knowing it He sends us help, whether an angel or friend, He is faithful and is constantly watching over us. Sometimes in the spiritual and sometimes a miracle in the natural world, our God cares for us. There is nothing that He will not do for us. After all, not only is He our Savior, Lord, and King but He is also our Amazing Big Brother.

"The righteous cry out, and the LORD hears, And delivers them out of all their troubles. The LORD is near to those who have a broken heart, And saves such as have a contrite spirit. Many are the afflictions of the righteous, But the LORD delivers him out of them all."

-Psalms 34:17-19 NKJV

Let brotherly love continue. Do not forget to entertain strangers, for by so doing some have unwittingly entertained angels.

-Hebrews 13:1-2 NKJV

"When you pass through the waters, I will be with you; And through the rivers, they shall not overflow you. When you walk through the fire, you shall not be burned, Nor shall the flame scorch you."

-Isaiah 43:2 NKJV

MY WALLET RETURNED

In August of 2011, I graduated from Teen Challenge and was called into the Dean of Men's office at the Benedict Castle in Riverside, headquarters of Southern California Teen Challenge where I was asked if I would take a rough position serving as an intern at the Los Angeles Teen Challenge men's home in Lynwood California where I would be trained to be a leader and eventually a staff member. Lynwood California is a very rough area next to Compton and as I got a few weeks into my internship I noticed a lot of sirens, a lot of gunshots at night, and helicopters flying around with huge spotlights canvassing around the neighborhood where we were, but I was always at peace knowing The Lord protected us.

I took the position and as I began to pray and ask The Lord for His direction, where I would be going after my 3-month Internship was over, The Lord spoke to me telling me I would be going to Bible College at the Teen Challenge Ministry Institute in South Gate California. That I would be going in December. I began to call the college to let them know I wanted to attend school there and that began the process of enrolling and within a couple of months after I received a call telling me that I was accepted but that I would not be able to get in right away because the waiting list had me in line for March, as other students were waiting to get in as well.

My three-month internship would be ending in November

and that meant I would have to do an extended internship in Los Angeles which didn't make any sense to me because I knew that the Lord had told me I would be going to TCMI in December. I prayed and I said to the Lord I knew that somehow He had already made a way for me and even though I was hearing others suggestions that maybe I hadn't heard the Lord right or maybe He had meant something else, I knew for sure in my heart what The Lord had said, that He was sending me there in December. I graduated my internship in November and a couple of weeks after I started my extended internship I got a phone call from TCMI telling me that they had some students drop out and I was moved up on the waiting list and would be attending in December just as The Lord had said.

I received a final call to come over and in the latter part of December, I packed my things and headed over to TCMI where I would spend the next year going to school. The day I arrived I was met by a staff member who walked me to my dorm and showed me the bunk I would be sleeping on and where I could unpack all of my things. I was told the college was pretty much empty, that no students were there and only a couple of staff members because everybody was on Christmas vacation at home with their families. I made my bed on the top bunk next to the back door of the building and the staff member came back in to check on me and gave me some rules.

He also let me know that the college dorms had been broken into a few times in the past during holiday break so to make sure to lock the doors at night. I finished unpacking my things and that night as Lance had directed me, I went around to all the doors and made sure they were locked then climbed up into my bed to go to sleep. I woke up in the middle of the night around 3 am, it was freezing cold and I looked over at the door next to my bed, to my surprise it was halfway open. I jumped down off my bunk closed the door and stood there for a few seconds listening. I didn't hear anything but I felt as if something was wrong, so I flipped on the light switch and walked around the building but it was empty.

I turned off the lights and went back into bed and when I got up in the morning I was shocked to find that when I put my pants on I reached into my pocket and my wallet was gone. I had folded my pants over the chair so I looked around some more but to my dismay, it was gone. I walked out of the dorm to the office to let the intern who was working there what had happened and he walked with me to the dorm and around the back of the building where he had locked up his bike. To his dismay, the bike was gone and only a cut lock and chain remained on the ground next to where his bike had been. We were both really mad about what had happened, especially since the staff there had told me about break-ins and it was my first night sleeping in my new home and I get robbed.

The intern said he had just bought his bike a week earlier and we both had a lot to say about this person who had ripped us off. I had to have my ID to do final enrollment as soon as the other students got back from vacation and knew it would take weeks to get a new one once I got to the DMV to order a replacement. Holy Spirit spoke to me at that very moment and asked me why not pray for this person who robbed us and remember where you came from when you were lost on drugs and didn't know Jesus. It softened my heart and I asked the intern if he wanted to pray with me and as we asked The Lord to save this person, to have mercy on them and that they would know Jesus my anger left and I felt peace.

I walked away out into the parking lot alone and just as many times before I took this situation to My Father asking Him for help and confirming my trust in Him that He would help me and meet my need for a new ID. As I finished praying I walked toward the front of the Bible College up the sidewalk toward the office and in the distance, I could see a guy pushing an elderly woman in a wheelchair and as they got closer to me the guys face was very downcast and the woman looked very sad and so when they got to where I was standing I smiled and asked how they were doing. The guy said not very well and began to tell me what he was going through. He said he was a member of the Church on our campus and he needed prayer because like those of us who went through Teen Challenge he was struggling with drug addiction and wanted to be free.

His mom who was in the wheelchair began to tear up and it really touched my heart because she loved her son very much and wanted him to be free from drugs and whole again. We all held hands and asked The Lord to help this brother and deliver him and that God would intervene. After we prayed he began to tell me a story the night before about a guy coming over to his house late at night, he had found a woman's purse on the street and had noticed the woman's Identification was inside, so he told the guy to return the purse and The Lord would bless him for doing the right thing for this woman. Right then I felt the presence of The Holy Spirit and a still small voice telling me that He would return my wallet to me. I was so blown away and as I walked away from this family I began to wonder how God would do this thing.

This was a few days before Christmas and every person I came into contact with at the College I told them what God had said to me. With anticipation, I called over to the Lynwood Teen Challenge center to tell them what had happened and to be on the lookout for someone to bring my wallet by. My ID had the address of that center on it because that is where I was living at the time and I figured in my mind someone would bring it by there, but God had something more amazing and incredible He was about to show me. On Christmas night after Church service I was standing in the same spot where I had prayed with that family on the phone with a friend explaining what God had said to me and as soon as the words came out of my mouth "The Lord is gonna bring my wallet back to me" this lady in a bright green shirt comes walking around the corner and looks at me and asks me my name, I tell her Tim and she says to me I have something that belongs to you.

To my amazement, she opens a black bag, reaches inside, and pulls out my wallet.

I cannot even describe how incredible and blown away I was at what was taking place right in front of my eyes but it launched my faith in such a powerful way, even to this day just giving this testimony I'm blown away at how Awesome and Incredible Our God Is and His ways of showing us He loves us and cares always amaze me. The only question I had left I asked this woman, how did you know you could find me here and she said that some gang members in her neighborhood had thrown my wallet with all its contents across her front lawn and she went around and picked everything up and just happened to have it in her bag walking around the neighborhood and recognized me from the picture on the ID. I thank you Lord that you are so amazing and gracious and I pray that all who read this testimony will experience something spectacular in their lives to launch their Faith in You and show them how much You Love them. The Lord Bless You All.

"For your Father knows the things you have need of before you ask Him."

-Matthew 6:8 NKJV

"And since we have the same spirit of faith, according to what is written, "I believed and therefore I spoke," we also believe and therefore speak, knowing that He who raised up the Lord Jesus will also raise us up with Jesus, and will present us with you. For all things are for your sakes, that grace, having spread through the many, may cause thanksgiving to abound to the glory of God."

-II Corinthians 4:13-15 NKJV

"Now thanks be to God who always leads us in triumph in Christ, and through us diffuses the fragrance of His knowledge in every place."

-II Corinthians 2:14 NKJV

THE PROMISE OF A DAUGHTER GIVEN

In 2012 while attending the Teen Challenge Ministry Institute in South Gate Los Angeles, I was given a promise by The Lord, and here's how it came to pass. Before fundraising we would stop off at a mall in the city we were fundraising, and this particular week I noticed an unusual number of men walking through the mall holding the hands of their little girls, laughing and smiling, having a good time. I sensed so much love in their relationship and for some reason it was wrenching my heart, almost bringing me to tears because it was so precious and because I wanted so much to be a daddy and to have a family. As we left the mall and got into the van I looked over at my driver Denise and I told her that if I ever had a little girl I would name her Hannah.

We went on that day fundraising as normal and we got home that night just like every other night ate dinner and went to bed. I walked out the door of the dorm that morning to go to breakfast just like I did every other day and as I walked down the sidewalk I made a left hand turn to walk past the community service office and the fundraising office when The Lord told me to stop. For some reason, the community service door was closed. Every other day that door would have been open and there would have been an intern sitting inside at a desk signing people in that were working off their community service there at T.C.M.I. This particular day though the intern was out sick.

There was a piece of paper taped to the middle of the door and it was the sign-in sheet. When the Lord told me to stop it was right in front of that door and I looked over on that piece of paper and saw one name, and that name was Hannah. I knew right then and there that God was telling me that I was going to have a daughter named Hannah and I was so blown away. I was so excited that God was going to bless me with a family and after praying about it several times and the Lord confirming to me that what I had seen was true, I began to dream about the future, what it was going to look like. It was like a dream but I knew that what God had said to me was going to come to pass and it was real. I had a sister in Christ named Micaela at that time, we didn't know each other that well but I remember she had the most amazing smile and was always laughing in good spirits.

She graduated three months before me and went off to work for Teen Challenge on the big island of Hawaii and when I graduated The Lord sent me to Hawaii as well to work for Teen Challenge in Honolulu. While in Hawaii in 2013 the doctors told Micaela that she would never have children because she had suffered a severe case of endometriosis for many years, a medical condition that she battled since she was 12 years old. She visited the doctor's office in Hawaii after suffering a really painful episode of her condition and after the doctors performed some tests, they told her that her ovaries were damaged and they advised her to have them removed.

Micaela and I remained friends after working for Teen Challenge, we would talk on the phone and a couple of times met up to just talk and hangout. I eventually moved back to California and we stayed in contact. One night she called to tell me she had told me how the doctors had just told her that she needed to have her ovaries removed and although I had already started having feelings for her, I thought to myself that I better stop pursuing anything more than friendship with her because I knew what The

Lord had promised me, that I was going to have a daughter and if Micaela could not have children, I assumed she was not the one The Lord would have planned for me in the future. Man makes plans but the Lord directs his steps.

I had no idea but The Lord was about to do an incredible miracle and bring amazing Glory out of this bad medical report. In 2015 Micaela got pregnant and 5 months later when we went to the doctor to find out if it was a boy or girl, the nurse showed us the sonogram and it was Hannah. We were both in awe of what the Lord had made possible. The Lord fulfilled a promise to me through Micaela after the doctors called her barren and Hannah our baby girl was coming into the world. Hannah was born on February 25th, 2016. Ten months later in December Micaela conceived again and our baby boy Christian was born on September 19th, 2017, another gift and miracle from The Lord.

A few months after Christian was born, Micaela and I discussed her getting surgery so that she could be healed of the pain that she suffered for many years due to her endometriosis. We went to the doctor and he told us that it would be a pretty safe procedure and we had nothing to worry about. So after praying we decided it was the right thing to do to help her be freed from her suffering and so she would have the surgery. In March 2018 Micaela had the procedure, a full hysterectomy, and two weeks later we were asked to come in for a follow-up.

The doctor who performed the surgery sat down with us and explained that it was a miracle that Micaela had two children, and without any complications at all. The doctor said that her ovaries were abnormal in size and that they were full of cysts. That her uterus was scarred with 2 inches of scar tissue on the inside wall of her bladder. It was an absolute miracle from God and we praise The Lord Jesus Christ for His incredible gifts of Hannah and Christian. Without a doubt, Jesus is still doing miracles today. Hannah and Christian are both perfectly healthy and have been such a blessing to our lives. Thank You Jesus for completing our family.

"Therefore it is of faith that it might be according to grace, so that the promise might be sure to all the seed, not only to those who are of the law, but also to those who are of the faith of Abraham, who is the father of us all (as it is written, "I have made you a father of many nations") in the presence of Him whom he believed—God, who gives life to the dead and calls those things which do not exist as though they did; who, contrary to hope, in hope believed, so that he became the father of many nations, according to what was spoken, "So shall your descendants be." And not being weak in faith, he did not consider his own body, already dead (since he was about a hundred years old), and the deadness of Sarah's womb. He did not waver at the promise of God through unbelief, but was strengthened in faith, giving glory to God, and being fully convinced that what He had promised He was also able to perform."
                                    -Romans 4:16-21 NKJV

Now indeed, Elizabeth your relative has also conceived a son in her old age; and this is now the sixth month for her who was called barren. For with God nothing will be impossible."
                                    -Luke 1:36-37 NKJV

Jesus looked at them and said, "With men it is impossible, but not with God; for with God all things are possible."
                                    -Mark 10:27 NKJV

PROVISION FROM HEAVEN

One morning after dropping off Hannah and Christian at Daycare, as I got on the freeway I noticed smoke was coming from the front of the car. It was getting worse as I drove along and I decided I had better get off and try to find a place to stop the car. As I rushed to get off the road I pulled into the first driveway I could find and when I got out of the car I knew our car was not going anywhere. There was green coolant pooling up under the front of the car and I thought the radiator must have cracked. We were in big trouble, stranded in the middle of town and we had only eight dollars to our name. Micaela and I had been through so much the last year and this was the last thing we needed on top of everything else. I knew the only thing I could do was pray and ask The Lord for help.

We had just in the last month moved and settled in El Paso Texas and didn't have a whole lot of options to get our car fixed, we didn't know anyone except some staff members at a rescue mission, and a couple of brothers and sisters from Church, so I prayed and felt Holy Spirit impress on my heart to call The Pastor of our new church. Pastor Steve from the first day we met was so loving and kind to us and Micaela and I had not experienced the Love of Jesus in such a powerful way as this man was showing toward us since the day we arrived in El Paso. He answered his phone and as I told him what had happened He immediately told us not to worry, He would send a tow truck to us and have it towed to a mechanic shop that he had done business with in the past.

I was blown away, The Lord was taking care of us, and not only that but Pastor Steve told us he would have the mechanic look over our car and find out what was wrong with it. We had no idea what was about to take place but it was another incredible testimony we would remember for the rest of our lives, one we would share, of the amazing Love and Faithfulness of God. So the most amazing part of this whole story is that the day before as Micaela and I were going to pick up a couple of things at Walmart, as we were pulling into the parking lot Micaela pointed out a woman on the sidewalk who was praying for a homeless man and we both were happy to see this sister ministering to him, we always appreciate seeing other believers doing good to those who are down and in need of The Love of Jesus.

So as we parked and walked into Walmart we were inside shopping around about 15 minutes when we turned a corner to go down the next aisle and run into the same lady who was praying for that man when we pulled in. Micaela struck up a conversation with her and we were amazed because this woman said she was just in town for a couple of days, that she and her husband were truck drivers, for more than twenty years, and just so happened Micaela and I had decided we were going to step out in faith the week prior and I was contacting different schools so that I could obtain a CDL and start truck driving.

The lady was excited for us and as we prayed together said that she wanted us to meet her husband so he could encourage us and give us information that would help us prepare for our new adventure truck driving across the country. We exchanged phone numbers and that night she invited us to lunch the next day to meet with her and her husband. Just so happens the next morning our car breaks down and there's a Denny's restaurant where they decide to come to meet us. They offered to drive us back to the rescue mission in their big rig after we had lunch, even to pick up Hannah and Christian from daycare which was a blessing as well. Hannah and Christian would be so excited to ride in the big truck...As we sit down to eat lunch, Danny, Margaret's husband starts to tell us all about his life truck driving, the ups and downs, and everything we could expect in the years ahead. It was great, we were very encouraged and knew it was what we wanted to do.

So as we were finishing up with our meal, Danny reaches across the table and hands me the change from a hundred dollar bills and tells me they also want to bless us with some money in our bank account to help us out. So on Sunday at church, I put ten percent into the offering, and the next day when we went to pick up the car from the mechanic's shop we were told it was paid and it was exactly ten times the amount to the penny of what I gave the day before..... Amazing Provision and Faithfulness of God.

Bring all the tithes into the storehouse, That there may be food in My house, And try Me now in this," Says The Lord of hosts, "If I will not open for you the windows of Heaven And pour out for you such blessing That there will not be room enough to receive it.

-Malachi 3:10 NKJV

Abraham called the name of that place The Lord Will Provide, as it is to this day, "In the Mount of The LORD it will be provided."

-Genesis 22:14 NKJV

Give, and it will be given to you: good measure, pressed down, shaken together, and running over will be put into your bosom. For with the same measure that you use, it will be measured back to you."

-Luke 6:38 NKJV

JESUS CHRIST IS LORD

Giving your life to Jesus Christ, putting your faith and trust in Him alone is a decision only you can make. It is the most important decision you will ever make in your life. Your eternal destination hangs right now at this very moment in a balance by the decision you make concerning the message of salvation you are hearing. "Today Is The Day Of Salvation". If you would like to know the Love of God and begin a true relationship with Jesus Christ, you can start by calling on Him right now in prayer, asking Him to come into your life, to be your Lord and Savior.

"The word is near you, in your mouth and in your heart" (that is, the word of faith which we preach): that if you confess with your mouth the Lord Jesus and believe in your heart that God has raised Him from the dead, you will be saved. For with the heart one believes unto righteousness, and with the mouth confession is made unto salvation. For the Scripture says, "Whoever believes on Him will not be put to shame." For there is no distinction between Jew and Greek, for the same Lord over all is rich to all who call upon Him. For "whoever calls on the name of the Lord shall be saved."
-Romans 10:8-13 NKJV

"Then Jesus said to His disciples, "If anyone desires to come after Me, let him deny himself, and take up his cross, and follow Me. For whoever desires to save his life will lose it, but whoever loses his life for My sake will find it."
Matthew 16:24-25 NKJV

PRAYER

{Father I want to know You. I believe You sent Jesus, to die as payment for my sins. I believe You raised Him from the dead so that I could have Eternal Life. I confess to You that I have sinned against You and I'm asking You to forgive me of all my sin and cleanse me from all unrighteousness. I confess to you today that Jesus Christ is Lord. Lord Jesus, come into my life now and be My Savior and Lord. I give my life to You. Baptize me and fill me with Your Holy Spirit and empower me to live a holy and blameless life. It's in Your Name Lord Jesus I pray, Amen}

   If you just prayed that prayer from your heart, and you have made a decision to follow Jesus Christ and live for God, you are now on the road to eternal life. I encourage you to tell someone right away about your New Life in Christ and also to find a Bible-believing church. I also encourage you most importantly to get a Bible and begin reading in the New Testament. Spend time in God's Word. The LORD Bless You......

"He who dwells in the secret place of the Most High Shall abide under the shadow of the Almighty. I will say of the LORD, "He is my refuge and my fortress; My God, in Him I will trust." Surely He shall deliver you from the snare of the fowler And from the perilous pestilence. He shall cover you with His feathers, And under His wings you shall take refuge; His truth shall be your shield and buckler. You shall not be afraid of the terror by night, Nor of the arrow that flies by day, Nor of the pestilence that walks in darkness, Nor of the destruction that lays waste at noonday. A thousand may fall at your side, And ten thousand at your right hand; But it shall not come near you. Only with your eyes shall you look, And see the reward of the wicked. Because you have made the LORD, who is my refuge, Even the Most High, your dwelling place, No evil shall befall you, Nor shall any plague come near your dwelling; For He shall give His angels charge over you, To keep you in all your ways. In their hands they shall bear you up, Lest you dash your foot against a stone. You shall tread upon the lion and the cobra, The young lion and the serpent you shall trample underfoot. "Because he has set his love upon Me, therefore I will deliver him; I will set him on high, because he has known My name. He shall call upon Me, and I will answer him; I will be with him in trouble; I will deliver him and honor him. With long life I will satisfy him, And show him My salvation.""

-Psalms 91:1-16 NKJV

Printed in the United States
By Bookmasters